dante's paradox

dante's paradox
A MEMOIR

DANTE M. SLATER SR.
CO-WRITTEN BY BRIDGET MAY

Dante's Paradox

Copyright © 2024 by Dante M. Slater Sr.

All rights reserved.

No part of this publication may be reproduced, distributed, or transmitted in any form or by any means, including photocopying, recording, or other electronic or mechanical methods, without the prior written permission of the publisher, except in the case of brief quotations embodied in critical reviews and certain other noncommercial uses permitted by copyright law.

Edited by Bridget May
Book design and layout by Jodi McPhee
Cover photograph by Michael Jones, Best Photographer Ever

ISBN: 979-8-9897389-0-8 (Paperback)
ISBN: 979-8-9897389-1-5 (eBook)

Printed in the United States

I dedicate this page to humanity,
as I love every last one of you.

"We are here on earth to do good to others.
What the others are here for, I do not know."

–Matthew Arnold

Contents

Acknowledgments xi
Foreword: Exploring the Uncharted Realms of Experience xiii
Preface xvii
Introduction 1
Chapter One: Haunted Houses 9
Chapter Two: Same Same 15
Chapter Three: Mother's Day 19
Chapter Four: Where's Brother? 25
Chapter Five: The Connection 29
Chapter Six: Peeking at the Future 35
Chapter Seven: Soccer's Lightning 39
Chapter Eight: The Birds 45
Chapter Nine: The Answer 51
Chapter Ten: Death Chronicles 55
Chapter Eleven: Just Missed It 61
Chapter Twelve: On My Mind 65
Chapter Thirteen: Not Kathy?! 69
Chapter Fourteen: Las Vegas 73
Chapter Fifteen: The Matriarch 79
Chapter Sixteen: In Closing: The One Percent DNA/
    Omniscience/Unity Consciousness/Love 87

Acknowledgments

I would like to begin by thanking my immediate support network, the small group of people who have been unwavering in their support of this book: Carolyn Slater and Timothy Horton for inspiring and encouraging me to write about these life experiences, who simply thought the story had meaning and needed to be told. I am humbled by their belief in and support of me.

Along with my wife, Kimberly (who at times is still mystified), whose willingness to let me run my course has enabled me to follow my dreams, and I love her truly for her selflessness.

I also would like to thank my children for showing me the traits I recognize in myself in them. Hopefully they realize how much they have taught me.

I am also grateful for my editor and ghostwriter, Bridget May. She came out of nowhere and made this writing thing a whole lot easier. More than a ghostwriter, Bridget deserves the title of co-writer. I wouldn't have it any other way.

I would like to thank all the Slater family for their incredible intuition and love, as well as my extended families, the Nettles's and Brannon's, throughout the years.

I also must acknowledge all friends, co-workers, etc…anybody I have had a conversation or connection with throughout my life (from the cradle to the grave).

You all are the reason I have made it thus far. I deeply appreciate all of you for what you brought into my life, no matter how brief.

From the bottom of my heart, thank you.

–Dante M. Slater

Foreword: Exploring the Uncharted Realms of Experience

LIFE OFTEN UNFOLDS in unexpected and uncharted ways. It is a journey that takes us through the realms of joy and sorrow, success and failure as we live out our days. But there exists another dimension, a realm often overlooked or dismissed as mere whimsy—a realm I was asked to explore in this captivating project.

When I was approached to contribute to this book, delving into the "woo-woo" subjects of premonitions, intuition, unexplained connections, and messages from enigmatic sources, my curiosity was piqued. It's a terrain we navigate personally and quietly, occasionally sharing stories in hushed tones, afraid of being labeled eccentric or dismissed as fanciful. Yet, as I began working with Dante on this project, I quickly realized the profound importance of embracing and understanding these experiences.

His narratives are not just anecdotes but windows into a world that exists beyond our conventional understanding.

Through his experiences, one can understand that the threads connecting us to the mysterious and the inexplicable are woven intricately into the fabric of our existence.

In a society that often prioritizes the tangible and the scientifically explainable, we find ourselves hesitating to share the moments when our intuition whispered truths, when premonitions urged us to alter our course, or when unexplainable connections offered solace in times of adversity. I think this stems from the fear of being labeled as believers in the supernatural, but in reality, these experiences are part of the collective human experience, silently connecting us all.

Dante's stories resonate with a universal truth—the recognition that there is more to life than meets the eye. As I delved into his narratives, I found myself reflecting on my own encounters with the unexplained, moments when my intuition guided me through the fog of uncertainty or when it provided profound insights that seemingly came from nowhere.

This book invites you, the reader, to embark on a journey beyond the conventional, to explore the seldom trodden paths of existence that extend beyond the boundaries of reason. It is a collection of stories that invites you to consider the possibility that our connection to the mysterious is an inherent part of being human, which is often overshadowed by the relentless pursuit of the material and the rational.

These narratives are not intended to provide irrefutable evidence or to convert skeptics into ardent believers. Instead, they serve as a testament to the richness and diversity of the human experience. Each story is a brushstroke on the canvas of the extraordinary, inviting us to contemplate the vastness of our own consciousness and the interconnectedness that binds us to all things.

We invite you to consider the possibility, and to open a dialogue, a space for reflection and discussion about the often-dismissed aspects of life, that when approached with an open mind may hold keys to understanding our purpose, our connections to each other, and the mysterious forces that shape our journey.

As you turn the pages of this book, may you find inspiration to embrace the uncharted realms of your own experiences. May you recognize that these narratives have the potential to reveal the extraordinary within your own life. I hope you enjoy this exploration into the unknown as much as I have, and that it sparks a newfound appreciation for the mysterious threads that bind us all.

–Bridget May
December 2023

Preface

I wrote this book because of the trauma I see people experiencing and dealing with every day.

Like most people, I've witnessed some terrible things happen to friends, family, co-workers, and associates. All sorts of catastrophic events—from tragic accidents, to spending time in jail for something they didn't do, to losing everything and being homeless in a matter of weeks, to being stricken with a terrible disease or affliction. It's traumatic and difficult to understand, especially when upon hearing the news you don't know what to say, unsure of which words will offer comfort.

It's the ones diagnosed with serious disease that touch me the most and make me wonder what they believe in. I find myself thinking a lot about the friends and family that have cancer. Do they have any speculation about what's next if they don't make it? Is their thinking permanently altered about life and their place in it if they win that battle?

I knew a person who had cancer which they fought and won, but when it came back some time later, they decided not to do a second round of treatment and subsequently died because of it. I could not understand why, if they beat it once, would they not do it again? What changed?

Another friend lost her son to a fentanyl overdose three years ago, and is still deeply grief-stricken.

My goal is to take her, friends with cancer, and people struggling with life's chaos and unfairness to another place intellectually. By offering a different perspective, some enlightenment if you will, and encouragement to look deeper, letting them know they are not alone.

My nephew Tim says I'm trying to close a gap. Yes, I think I found a small piece of the missing piece in the puzzle and I want to share it with everyone. This is all a process and we have to trust it. Hopefully I can offer some fresh eyes.

–Dante Slater

dante's paradox

Introduction

"Let go of certainty. The opposite isn't uncertainty. It's openness, curiosity and a willingness to embrace paradox, rather than choose up sides. The ultimate challenge is to accept ourselves exactly as we are, but never stop trying to learn and grow."

–Tony Schwartz

If there's one thing I know for sure, it's that watching your children grow up and evolve as humans, recognizing various family traits and influences, is fascinating if you pay attention.

I feel lucky enough that I paid attention to my daughter, Marquette, as she grew up. Her curiosity to try everything, and intelligence to figure it out, made her a natural learner, but I dreaded the day she would ask what our purpose in life was. After all, I wasn't sure I even knew my purpose yet.

Sure, every year brought a little more clarity, but it also brought more of my own awareness that when it came down to it, the more I saw and experienced, that there was a lot I didn't know as well. I was grateful that we did not have that conversation until she was 25.

It's taken me about that long to see that acts of service to our fellow humans are probably the most important purpose in life. Whether it's working for the school district like her mom and grandmother, gaining qualifications in education—a PhD like one aunt, or gaining a doctorate like another, or getting a bachelors in education like her cousin—or becoming a psychiatrist like her aunt, my family's strong tradition of helping others is not something that's taught; maybe it's just in our bloodline. Even Marquette herself is a behavioral technician working in the school system. By the time she became an adult, Marq's natural helping tendencies were apparent and it was an easier conversation to have. Life is still not always what it appears to be.

According to Oxford Languages (the world's leading dictionary publisher):

A **paradox** is a seemingly absurd or contradictory statement or proposition, that when investigated or explained may prove to be well founded or true.
"In a paradox, he has discovered that stepping back from his job has increased the rewards he gleans from it."
◆ A statement or proposition that, despite sound (or apparently sound) reasoning from acceptable premises, leads to a conclusion that seems senseless, logically unacceptable, or self-contradictory.
"A potentially serious conflict between quantum mechanics and the general theory of relativity known as the information paradox."
◆ A situation, person or thing that combines contradictory features or qualities.
"The mingling of deciduous trees with elements of desert flora forms a fascinating ecological paradox."

Basically it's just something that is opposed to common sense or logic but turns out to be true.

There are a whole host of specific paradoxes under that umbrella that most of us are familiar with.

All of them can make your head spin if you think about them too much.

Sometimes I feel like my whole life has been like that definition. Attempting to discover the truth of a thought or situation that defies logic.

The way I see it is that on one hand there is the world "out there:" work, school, university, church, society, making money, social media, TV, sports, nature, etc. Let's say this makes up 99 percent of our consciousness and our time. It is mostly how things "are." What we are told is true and real and what is not. Things that easily make sense.

But on the other hand, there is the "inner world" we all have, which is a mash of personal observation, genetics, beliefs, habits, education, thoughts, generational influence, feelings, and all the other indefinable things that make up being human. I think this is a look into the remaining one percent.

The things that seem so far-fetched, almost ridiculous, yet are so commonplace that almost everyone you know has experienced the events or knows someone that has had an experience with one of them.

Depending on the mindset of the dominant person in the experience, most of these events go undefined; just a "thing" that everyone chooses to explain away, or ignore, or classify as "a coincidence." Many of these experiences cannot be explained by science either because they cannot be recreated in a controlled environment. They fall into the paradox classification: seemingly simple at first glance, but upon closer inspection, the logic is curious. Like, everyone knows, if you travel back in time, you should definitely not kill your grandparent as you might create some time-paradox-rift in the timeline. But if you go back and prevent yourself from being born, how are you even able to time travel in the first place? This is the grandfather paradox and it really does make you think in circles.

The universe holds so much more knowledge than we can only hope to understand in our day-to-day lives. As humans, we know a lot (the 99 percent), but we don't know everything (the one percent).

In the U.S., we are taught from childhood that being a consumer is the most important thing. Most of us spend our days on a treadmill of survival: commuting, working, spending money, and trying to get the next thing we are told we need, be it a newer car, updated phone, or whatever.

In normal day-to-day life, we are not encouraged to veer off course and entertain anything that is a little odd. And if we do touch on these experiences, these conversations barely go beyond random speculation with people we deem smarter than us in these matters, usually those with a scientific background or our local clergy or minister.

Some people are satisfied with the answers that science or religion have to offer, but I have noticed that there is a curiosity amongst other people, concerning a number of situations and events, that do not fit the scientific or even religious narrative at times.

I feel like I've seen a lot of those events, and they seem simple enough, until I try to explain them to someone else, or ask someone who has experienced such events with me to talk about it. Often it is difficult and they can't arrive at a satisfactory personal explanation, so they shut it out.

But it's the one percent that gives it all meaning. The connections we experience with our loved ones, and the world we live in, the signs and symbols from the natural world and the universe, are all around us all the time. What makes them connect to us? What connects us to the earth? Or our families, and communities?

I think it's because we are all energy, with all of us projecting electrical vibrations, like radio towers, sending out and receiving signals at all times.

Is it any wonder that the people closest to us can alert us to big things that happen without words, things that are powerful and cause us to send strong signals like s.o.s waves out into the universe?

Is it any wonder that we are tuned into these people or pick up on these signals? It makes sense that some people are particularly sensitive to these signals and understand them with ease. Some people are sensitive to these signals and do not understand them so easily. Sometimes the events are disturbing and upsetting.

So then, is it too much of a reach to detect disturbances before they happen?

Considering our inherent abilities to perceive feelings of connection to the natural world, is it so unbelievable that such energy could transmit from the future? Precognition? Knowledge that something good or bad will happen? Or a nudge to do something? Dreams that show us an event in the future? The urge to reach out to friends or loved ones we have not seen for a long time? Or not leave at the usual time? Or take a different road? The urge to give someone a random piece of advice?

There are hundreds of recorded events in history from all corners of the world, from all sorts of people from all positions in life, who changed their plans last minute because they felt a strong urge to not do something—catch a flight, or get on a boat or a train, take the trip, or do any number of planned activities, which ended up saving their lives. Although there is no accepted scientific evidence that precognition is real, there is enough anecdotal evidence that says it is.

So then, who is right? The people who are still alive because they listened to their gut and didn't do something? Or the people trying to recreate the validity of the authentic situation in a controlled environment?

We have all seen and felt things that we often put down to coincidence, a seemingly inconsequential event, an impulse to do something seemingly random, a clear voice in our head telling us to say something to someone, a similar dream, a flock of birds in an unexpected place. There is still so much which science cannot prove or investigate simply because the events can't be accurately recreated. If it seems potentially valid, they try, but without logic (theory), and evidence (observation), it's difficult to prove. Theory and observation are irrevocably intertwined in science and cannot exist without each other, thus discounting a multitude of events for those that only see in terms of science or religion.

Or what about having total memory recalls? It has been proven that our long-term memory can store a seemingly unlimited amount of information, with some researchers questioning if we ever forget anything, the problem being that we do not possess the capability to recall said stored memories as we demand. So experiencing an event where a complete memory is recalled at that seemingly inconsequential time is completely random.

But is it? How do we know it wasn't knowledge released by our subconscious to provide context to the situation we are about to, or did just experience? We know our brains are incredibly complex and plastic in nature. They are able to continually build new connections and neural pathways, and the brain does so much that we are unclear on, who's to say it doesn't reserve the knowledge for a later date, whether it's intellectual or emotional? Or that our subconscious accesses that information as it knows we will need it? It's these things that are fascinating to me as I recall events from my own life. I can't help but want to find satisfactory explanations. As a person who believes in science and universal knowledge, I know there must be a connection.

Telepathy, coincidence, multiple and parallel universes, total memory recall, spiritual awakenings, predestination, premonitions. Science has really only just begun to investigate such occurrences, or at least the ones that can be acknowledged. Many are still considered pseudoscience. There is little doubt these occurrences are true, especially if you are the one that experienced it. Often they just end up being a paradox; simple, yet not.

Many of us have experienced such occurrences as well, and like me, strive to figure out why they are true. What is the one percent, that inner world? The thing that holds it all together? The thing that gives everything meaning and is all around us and binds us to one another? What is the thing that connects us to people very strongly, in unseen ways? What creates life?

For me, the most obvious and often overlooked ingredient of all is love. Without it, there is nothing of meaning that happens between people. And most of these experiences happen between people who love each other and have or had a strong connection at some point. Like our energies imprint and entwine and we are forever connected. I often think, that in the case of close personal relationship dynamics, that the brains of the family will be in tune for a lifetime.

There have been many of these occurrences in my life, and I have documented them here as I explore my own paradoxes and attempt to make sense of these events. As a generally skeptical person, I have largely ignored them throughout my life—or not placed much importance on them—but I have realized there comes a point when you have to stop and look at these things because they don't go away. They are always there, the things that keep me awake in the middle of the night. Trying to figure out the connections and reasons, or even if they are related or just a random series of events, will drive a person to drink to escape it all.

I don't think life is just a random collection of events that happen to us though. I think we are all connected by love, to each other and to the universe. I think it is much more simple than we tend to make it.

The one percent shapes everything and nothing. All I can do is keep learning.

Chapter One
HAUNTED HOUSES

Throughout my childhood, I thought we always lived in haunted houses.

From a young age, I would be woken up regularly by shrieking sounds, high pitched screams, and demonic sounding whispers. These unearthly sounds of goblins, ghosts, demons, witches, and evil spirits would occur multiple times a week. It was like something out of the exorcist.

Looking back, I think that's probably why I wet the bed when I was very young. I would hear these sounds in the house and be terrified to get out of bed. Nobody knew why I heard these noises, or why they moved with us from house to house.

I was a very fearful child. It didn't help that my mother was a staunch Christian.

My mother was a multi-faceted and talented woman. As one of the lead soprano singers at our church, she had turned her hobby of dried floral arranging into a second source of income. She had a lot of energy and a lot of beliefs that shaped our lives. As a young child and into my early teens, she instilled in me a terrified distrust of almost everything outside of our four walls, immediate community, and family structure.

Mom believed in a vengeful God, and the fear of Our Lord Almighty was drilled into me. Evil was lurking around every corner and the devil was waiting to snatch my soul at any moment.

Which is exactly why I made the decision to raise my own child without religion. After spending years recovering from the fanatical fear that was pumped into me during my formative years, I decided my daughter did not need that too. Turns out my theory was correct. She is not worried or scared of the hypothetically horrible things religion fills you with fear about.

My daughter and I communicate about everything, and the natural instinct for a huge number of humans to automatically revert to fear is something we take issue with. Sure, it may have done us well in caveman times, but we do not need to surround ourselves with a community that continues to do so. And it is a choice to think that way. Keeping my daughter away from the zealots was a good decision for us.

Waking up in the middle of the night to these sounds was made all the more terrifying as I seemed to be the only one that heard them. It was a recurring waking nightmare, where night after night I would wake up in a cold sweat with my senses on high alert, my heart thumping so loudly I would think the demons and monsters would hear me and come and get me. Week after week, month after month, I never got used to it.

Occasionally, Mom would sleep in different rooms of our house, because she couldn't get comfortable in her own bed.

"There's someone in the house! There's someone else here!"

She would barely move and would say, "There's nobody in the house, boy. Go back to sleep."

Feeling safe momentarily with my mother's reassurance, I would drift back to a fitful sleep.

I dreaded each bedtime though. I never knew when the haunting would happen again.

One night, when I was about six years old, the entities (as I had started calling them) were extra loud. Their demonic chattering and urgent whispers, interspersed with mumbles and cackles and witchy-sounding laughter, was like a tidal wave of unbearable madness. I woke up terrified again, but decided I had had enough. I was going to find out what this was once and for all.

I summoned enough confidence to get out of bed and follow the noises. I was completely spooked. I was on such a high alert that I could hear my PJs move as I tiptoed down the hall and turned on the light as I got closer to the noises. They were coming from the spare room at the end of the hall. My legs felt stiff and heavy like they were made of concrete as I got closer to the door. The voices were very loud now, and it sounded like at least three beings were in there. I carefully pushed open the door and squinted through the darkness into the room. I hadn't noticed how bright the hall light was before, and staring into the pitch dark, I felt a single bead of cold sweat run down the side of my face.

It took a moment for my eyes to adjust. I was tense with fear expecting something or a few somethings to lunge at me. My skin was covered in goosebumps. Every hair on my body felt prickly.

In the semi darkness of the room, I could see there was someone laying on the bed. I looked around the dark room trying to make out the others, but there was just the one lone figure in the room, its head turning violently from side to side and mouth jabbering and heckling, its body shivering and shuddering. I pushed open the door wider so that the light from the hallway illuminated the bed and the figure. First I saw the feet moving and kicking, then the rest of the body became clear.

I nearly screamed with shock. *It was my own mother.* Thrashing and jabbering in a sleep trance.

"MOM?!" I yelled. "It's been you all the time?!"

The wave of relief and anger washed over me almost simultaneously, but was quickly replaced with utter confusion. What on earth? Our houses weren't haunted; it was Mom the whole time. I couldn't believe no one had told me about this!

From that point on, it would still scare the hell out of me, never knowing when she would have one of her sleep spells. Sometimes I could wake her up and she would stop. I would shake her and yell, "Mom, wake up! You're talking in your sleep again."

She would become conscious, sit up, look at me, and stop. Then she would lay back down and go back to sleep.

I would usually stand there for a minute, ready to wake her up if she started again. No matter how long I stood there, she would stay silent.

Yet as soon as I turned to head back to my room and walked through the door into the hall, she would let out a high-pitched squeal that would send tight shivers of fear up the back of my neck, making the hairs on my arms stand up. Every single time.

It was like she was possessed with a mischievous entity that delighted in scaring the crap out of me.

I would yell in frustration at her and sometimes she would stir and mumble.

Realizing how futile my efforts were, I would tip-toe back to my room and climb back into bed and make myself comfortable again. But, predictably, no sooner than I dropped back to sleep, she would start again, in full voice, like a fire alarm going off in your own house at 3:00 A.M.

As I grew older, it would still be a little bit scary, but mainly I would wake up frustrated and I would just yell from my room, "MOM! Wake up!"

She would answer, "Boy, shut up and go back to sleep."

Then I would hear a high-pitched, little witchy laugh, "Eh heh heh heh heh," making me wonder if it had been her that answered in her normal voice or one of the entities.

I hated it, and I thought for a while it had something to do with her eating collard greens and cornbread late at night, so I told her to stop eating so late.

Most nights I would just cover my ears with my pillow and bury myself deep in my bed. It felt like it would never end.

As an adult, I have learned more about sleep disorders and the things that can happen inside a person's brain while they move from one sleep cycle to another. They fall under the umbrella term of parasomnias. My mom definitely experienced sleep-talking, but thank goodness not sleep-walking, or any of the other seven identified parasomnias. And if we're getting further into the sleep-talking, which is called somniloquy, science hasn't spent a lot of time investigating the phenomena. They don't know why it happens or what is happening in the brain when it does. It is commonly believed to be harmless.

Everything I've read about sleep-talking to-date does not mention the voices and demonic chatter I would hear from her. Or the fact that at least one of the voices seemed to be aware when I was trying to make her stop. I often wondered if it was part of the reason that she was such a faithful member of her congregation. Did she know she did this? Was she possessed? An open channel to the spirit side? She never remembered the next day when I said anything, and she never let on if her parents or family members ever had those experiences either. I never thought to ask. I didn't want to know.

I think, on some level, she knew of these entities, whether it was part of her subconscious or a family curse, or part of a personality disorder that only displayed during sleep. And I think that was why she filled my head with so much fear and reverence for God, an attempt on her part to ward off whatever it was that pursued her. We were so close and very similar, I think as I was the baby of the family she was extra aware of all these things. She would make me feel like I had to say prayers and go to church with her, otherwise the devil would get me. I wonder if she thought that was what had her.

Looking back, I think she knew and she didn't want me to know. One of the regrets I have in my recollections of my relationship with her, is that I never asked her about it.

Chapter Two
SAME SAME

Just as I had similar or the same traits and perceptions as my mother did, I've noticed that my daughter, Marquette, and I experience the same aches and pains. Not just similar, but the exact same locations and limbs. For example, if my left eye was bothering me like I had something in it, I would get home and discover Marquette's left eye had been red and irritated all afternoon too. If my wrist was hurting, hers would be as well. Headache on one side of my head, she would have one in the same spot too. Rolled my ankle at work; she did it in gym class. This is a connection we have shared for most of her life, where we both end up with injuries or damage to the same parts of our bodies, often within the same time period, only to find out about the other one when we get home.

I had an infected foot once, but because of life and my work schedule, I had not said anything to my wife, as I figured it would just go away. Until one evening when I got home from work. I said something to my wife because it had gotten worse. "Which foot?" she asked. "My right foot." She looked at me, barely surprised and said, "Your daughter has been complaining of pain in her right foot too." The pain did not subside for either of us over the next few days and I ended up having to go to the emergency room when I couldn't get my foot into my work boot. The doctor told me if I had waited any longer they would have had to amputate it because the infection had spread. By this time, Marquette's right foot was infected too. We got her to the doctor a lot quicker than I had waited.

We have both also had surgery on our right toes.

It has always been this way. Even my wife isn't surprised by the coincidence anymore. And if Marquette told her she had a headache or toothache or anything, she'd ask about my tooth or head or whatever when I'd call her from work, knowing inevitably I would have some sort of issue there as well.

I used to think it was weird that my wife knew me so well she could tell if I was experiencing some sort of pain, but actually it was only because Marq had come home and told her that she had that pain. She saw a definite pattern with us, but it was so commonplace, like so many out-of-the-ordinary events that happen in people's daily lives, it had ceased to be extraordinary in our family.

To this day we still have the ridiculously similar ailments at the same time in the same area of the body; this has never gone away.

I've investigated this phenomenon a little to see if there is a telepathic or empathic connection between parents and their children's pain. I can't find anything that explains the connection I share with my daughter. The only thing that sort of comes close is the fabled bond that twins experience, but mainly that is because they are just so close emotionally and psychologically.

I would say I'm close to my daughter, but not "twin" close.

I have found out what it is *not* though. There is a wealth of information about psychosomatic causes, but it's not sympathy pains where one person experiences the pain they see a loved one experiencing (like pregnancy pains), because most of the time, it just starts or happens independently without knowledge of what's going on with each other until later.

It's not mirror-touch synesthesia where one person can experience a similar sensation (like touch) that they see happening to another person.

It's not trans-generational pain where if a parent has chronic pain issues, the child experiences them as well.

I've often wondered if it's a type of ESP that somehow runs through my family bloodline. That is one I'm still researching.

Like so many other things I have become aware of in my life, at the moment it's just "one of those things," part of the one percent for now.

Chapter Three
Mother's Day

One year, when I had hung out late the night before Mother's Day, my daughter came to me the next morning and asked, "Hey, Dad, what are we doing for Mom for Mother's Day?"

"Well, honey," I started, "it's just another day, you know."

Personally, I'm not a holiday or birthday person. I just don't see the point in celebrating one arbitrary day. I mean, if you can't be grateful and nice to the people you love every day, what difference is one day a year going to make? I think it just gives everyone permission to act the fool and disrespect each other the other 360-plus days a year, and as long as they make a big effort on that one day, that's OK? It just doesn't make sense to me.

She folded her arms. "But it's Mother's Day."

I shrugged. "We're not going to be doing much." She took exception to that, and she rolled her eyes at me, turned on her heel and left the room. I didn't think anything else of it, being more concerned with ridding myself of the hangover I had. I lay back down.

Before long I could hear her downstairs, opening and closing cupboards and drawers, rolls of paper being unraveled, cutting and chopping; the general sounds of creativity. I figured she must be doing a school project or something. Marquette was always doing her own thing.

After I heard this carry on for a while however, curiosity got the better of me and I went downstairs to see what she was doing.

She was almost finished making an incredibly intricate small flower arrangement for her mom for Mother's Day.

I was blown away by so much creativity in about thirty minutes. "Wow, Boop (my pet name for her), that's really cool. Did you remember that from art class when you went to elementary in Beaverton?"

"No, Dad, I never went to art class in Beaverton."

"Sure, you did," I replied, doubting my memories.

"No."

"Huh." I was positive that was where she must have learned it.

"My bad. Was it one of the things you learned in art class here in Vancouver then?"

She gave me that look that kids give their parents when they don't know what they're talking about and said, "No, I've never been to art class, Father." She went back to putting the finishing touches on the bouquet.

"Sure you have," I persisted.

Sometimes parents don't listen to their kids, with disastrous results. I didn't think this was one of those times though.

"Well, you must have learned it at Tigard then."

"Nope."

I could not let it go. In my head I thought there was no way she just made something so intricate and detailed out of thin air. She must have been taught or was shown by someone at some point. We went around and around with me suggesting places where she was shown this craft and her denying ever being taught anything in any art class, because she had never been to art class.

I decided to wait until her mother came home.

My wife returned from her trip to the coffee shop and Marquette gave her the tiny, intricate bouquet. She was very impressed and said it was the coolest thing she'd ever been given, and gave her a big hug. After our daughter had left the room, I brought it up with my wife.

"Hey, you know, Marquette doesn't think she went to art class in Beaverton, but I'm sure she went to art class in Oregon, right?" My wife shook her head. She was still turning the bouquet over in her hands, taking in every detail.

"Or in Washington?"

She lowered the bouquet for a moment, giving me a puzzled look.

"What are you talking about, Dante? She has never been to art class, anywhere."

"Huh." I didn't believe her.

I was still stuck on the art class thing, and I could tell by her short answers my wife thought I was crazy. We argued for a little while longer before I told her I would let it go.

But I didn't let it go.

Mentally I was still wondering where on earth she learned to make something that detailed and elaborate. Suddenly, I remembered an interesting documentary I had watched on PBS a few weeks beforehand, about how instinct and inherent knowledge are acquired in the natural world. That millions of pieces of hereditary information are attached to the sperm as it makes its way through the penis in the milliseconds before ejaculation. Which then combines with the millions of pieces of information in the egg. Just like in all of the animal kingdom. I remembered it clearly because I had been a little disappointed, thinking that as humans we were somehow superior in our passing along of chromosomes. But not really. In this instance we are no different than all birds, fish, and animals. Sperm meets egg, life begins.

I also remembered my early childhood, being in my mom's flower shop, the little shop with the distinct potpourri fragrance that hung in the air. She would show me how to make simple dried floral arrangements to keep me busy. I would try to make them perfect. She would laugh and tell me they couldn't look perfect because then they would not look real. Flowers don't naturally come together perfectly in horizontal, diagonal, or vertical patterns. They need to look real. My mother was very patient with her flowers. She had an eye for detail and constructed each piece with laser-like precision and focus.

So as I was thinking about Marquette's brand new self-taught skill, I was still blown away that in less than one hour she just figured it out on her own. A beautiful tiny floral bouquet made of paper. There was just no way she plucked that craft out of her imagination. And if she had never attended an art class, where did it come from? I couldn't help but draw a connection between the PBS documentary about hereditary information passed on to our children through chromosomes and DNA, and it made me wonder: If things like eye color and genetic predisposition to illness can be passed on, why not creative and artistic ability too? Is it science that can explain these things? More so than coincidence or spiritual influence? It gave me new depth to the thought that blood is thicker than water, even thicker than mud.

Chapter Four
WHERE'S BROTHER?

One summer it was really hot, and Marquette was sleeping in our room because hers didn't have AC. She was sleeping on the floor closest to the unit, in between our bed and the window. It was very early on a Sunday morning when my wife and I were woken up out of a dead sleep by Marquette yelling, "Where is brother at?!" in a very alarmed tone of voice.

My wife and I sat up simultaneously like the dead rising from coffins in those old horror movies, and Marquette was just leaning her chin on the bed staring at us with a strange look on her face. Her eyes were wide and she looked like she was looking into another dimension. It was eerie. She stared vacantly at us for about five seconds and then lay back down, instantly back asleep.

My wife leaned over our bed to look at her, saw she was sound asleep, and turned back to me. We looked at each other, confused and a bit freaked out.

What was that about? A dream? Nightmare? Was something wrong with her? We had more questions than answers and thought about waking her up, but decided it could wait until the morning.

It was about then I felt my hangover kicking, so I got up and headed downstairs for a glass of water. As I walked into the kitchen, our phone started ringing. The old house phone that hung on the wall was loud in the quiet kitchen, and I reached for it, vaguely wondering who would be calling us at this hour. I was still thinking about Marquette's sleep-talking, if that's what it was. But I was brought back in a hurry by my son's voice on the other end. He was upset and yelling erratically, something about how his girlfriend screwed him over, how they got in a fight, and he ended up in jail. He said I needed to go get him out.

I said, "OK, I'll come get you later. You need to calm down."

Dante Jr. sighed and said, "Put some money on my books if I don't get out of here," which struck me as a strange thing to say. He told me where he was; I told him he could use the time to cool off and that I'd pick him up later. By the time I hung up, he was calmer. As I drank the second glass of water, I stared at the ceiling.

I thought it was strange that Marquette woke up yelling about him only a couple of minutes before he called, somehow picking up on his distress while she was dreaming. This defied my basic habit of slotting things into convenient mental boxes. This was the one percent, and it was the first time I realized that my children and I possibly shared a connection. Some sort of telepathy. I didn't think I believed in that sort of thing, but I did check the bottle I had been drinking and poured it down the drain. Just in case.

Although, the fact that family members are connected to the extent that they can perceive each other's distress is not that much of a reach. There is plenty of anecdotal evidence of siblings and other family members picking up on each other's stress and trauma. Marquette has always been a very empathic person, and although Dante Jr. wasn't in the house for long when she was a child, they still shared a bond. So it's not too crazy to think that he sent out an SOS signal, being in a highly agitated and emotional state, and it reached her.

She didn't remember it happening the next day, and didn't believe us when we told her. She was truly like a radio receiver, crackling to life with a strong signal and then losing it again, never truly leaving her sound sleep.

This event defies science, and in my mind is an obvious connection to the one percent of life that we can't satisfactorily explain away.

Chapter Five
THE CONNECTION

I FELL INTO THE habit for a while where I would stop by the local gentleman's club. It was somewhere to drink heavily and try to take a few spins around the pole without getting cut off and thrown out. It became almost automatic, just a quick stop on the way home when I finished a 12-hour shift. Although the habit didn't last too long, I realized how easy it was to "forget" the important commitments I had. Things that were ten times more important to me than being drunk in such an establishment.

This was never more apparent to me than one night, after about nine drinks too many, I was doing my best to not get eighty-sixed, and Rage Against the Machine was playing. I remember thinking somewhere in my drunk mind that I hadn't expected to hear them in the background. I was sprawled over the stage with a dollar in my mouth, and I realized with a jolt of clarity that I had to go. The memory that I had one-on-one soccer practice with my daughter in the morning sobered me up fast enough to get home. As her coach, I knew practice was more important than whatever it was I thought I was doing, and besides, I looked forward to soccer.

The next morning we got up early and went to practice.

Like every parent teaching or coaching their own, I could be a bit hard on her sometimes. It's easy to transfer your adult expectations onto your kid. She wasn't fast like her mom, but I had encouraged her ambidextrous tendencies and she was strategically thoughtful like me. I had taught her how to play chess a couple of years before, and she knew it well. It was the perfect game for her strategic thinking.

But if she was as fast as her mom had been, I had no doubt she would easily be in the top twenty picks of her high school's athletes.

It was a good session though, and after practice we headed straight home, taking the same way that we always did. As we drove through the intersection that ran below the underpass not far from our apartment, there was a blur to the left of us of a car running the light at high speed, which T-boned us like a train and caused us to roll over several times, the sound of metal on metal, and breaking glass, and metal crunching and sliding was violent and intense. And we eventually came to a stop upside down in the middle of the street, right in front of our building. Our seat belts were holding us in place and I could see blood dripping from my head onto the roof below me. I looked over at Marquette, and to my surprise she was calm, just looking around at the whole situation.

I thought she must be in shock.

"Are you OK, Boop?"

Her eyes were very large and she replied with a very quiet, "Yes."

Terrified, I suddenly woke up in my own bed, dripping with sweat and gasping for air, my heart pounding in my ears. It was only a dream. An awful, terrible nightmare, but a dream all the same.

As I sat up, my wife was stirring, and at the same time Marquette let out a terrified yelp and called urgently for her mom. She sounded scared and upset. In an instant, my wife was awake, leaping out of bed and dashing out of the room.

I could still hear the screeching violent echoes of the crash in my head. I took a few deep breaths, and as I gathered myself, I decided I needed some water. I walked past Marquette's room, and I saw them sitting on the bed, our daughter wrapped in a big hug from her mom, while Marquette told her about the horrific nightmare. She had dreamed that she and I were in a violent car crash at the intersection only half a block from our building.

I was still sleep dazed and not entirely sure of what was real or not at this point. Was the crash real and this was the dream? Or was this real and the crash was the dream? In that strange, sleepy quiet and darkness of a house unexpectedly awake at 3:00 A.M., I was not sure. I went and got that water. I thought Marq probably needed some too.

After she cuddled with her mom for a little longer, I asked her to tell me the details of her nightmare, and she described in exact detail the nightmare I'd just had. Even down to the part where I was dripping blood onto the roof, and she looking around feeling calm.

She was incredibly disturbed by the nightmare, and she became even more unsettled realizing that I had experienced the same dream, at the same time.

So then I was even more confused.

How was that even possible? Why and how did we just have the exact same nightmare?[1] Was it a premonition of something that was going to happen to us in the future?

In the fifteen years since then, I have only driven alone in the car with her a handful of times. I was just too spooked by that dream to even risk it. Marquette, on the other hand, wasn't bothered at all.

When she was old enough to drive, she texted me once at the bar to tell me she would pick me up and take me home after I won some money. I said sure. But as soon as I hit send, the remembered trauma of that dream hit me, and I texted her right back to say not to worry as I found a ride. I was still spooked that we had experienced such a graphic and violent shared dream.

Looking into it though, I have learned that although shared dreaming is a recognized phenomenon that occurs between people with strong empathic relationships in spiritual communities and many other cultures around the world, it is rejected by mainstream science.

Carl Jung, the revolutionary Swiss psychiatrist and psychoanalyst who founded analytical psychology, had a controversial theory about the existence of a collective (or trans-personal) unconscious, that there is a possibility of a shared mind that connects everyone and even connects all time from present to the origins of the human species and beyond. This is definitely one percent stuff. So it makes sense that it is some sort of familial

---

[1] https://www.dreams.co.uk/sleep-matters-club/what-are-shared-dreams-2

connection. But what exactly did my mother pass down to me? It's hard to pinpoint when it was not something ever talked about when you were growing up.

All I *do* know is that the way I thought about and viewed everything was changing, and I began to question everything in life. Nothing was ever as it seemed. That one percent was showing up everywhere.

Chapter Six

PEEKING AT THE FUTURE

THROUGHOUT MOST OF our daughter's education, my wife, Kimberly, took Marquette to school in the mornings. The bus stop was several blocks away, but she figured if she had to get in the car to drive her half way there anyway, she may as well just take her the whole way. Besides, it was good to spend time with her in the morning. Every single day like clock work, they would leave at exactly the same time, and drive the same route.

Day in and day out, week after week, their routine was predictable: Kim would ask Marquette if she was ready by 7:10 A.M., and they were in the car and driving by 7:15 A.M. There was never a problem, and they were seldom late.

I can only think of two times they left the house late and Marq had to be signed in to school.

One morning, she was a little slow getting into the car. She forgot something and had to run back in to get it. When she got back to the car, she even said to Kim, "I don't know why I felt like I needed this today," which turned out to be for the best, for it was only a few minutes later they watched a big truck barrel through a red light just ahead of them, and realized that if they had been on time, they would have been passing through the intersection at that time. Marquette looked at her mom and said, "I knew something was going to happen this morning!" My wife agreed, but didn't think anything of it, and she only mentioned it in passing to me later as it wasn't a completely unusual sort of thing for Marq to say.

Another morning, Marquette was not ready. She was a little frustrated this particular morning. She couldn't find something she needed for school, and she didn't want any help, so Kim just went back into the kitchen and poured another cup of coffee. It didn't bother her if they were a few minutes late.

They left about five minutes later than usual. Marquette was still feeling irritated even after she found whatever it was that she had needed, because she didn't like being late. They were talking as they drove down the same streets, through the same intersections, past the store and all the regular landmarks. Everything was the same except they were a little over ten minutes late by then.

However, it wasn't long until traffic slowed and they were passed by several emergency vehicles at high speed with lights and sirens blaring. As they were approaching one of the main intersections, they could see all sorts of chaos ahead. There had been a serious roll-over accident and they could see one car on its side smoking, and another one across the other side so wrecked it was hard to tell which way it had been going. As they approached the scene, the car which was smoking burst into flames.

More emergency services were arriving at the same time as my wife and Marquette pulled up, and firemen were working on cutting a lady out of the flaming car. The woman was screaming so loudly and hysterically that Kimberly and Marquette could hear her from inside their own car. There was a state trooper directing traffic, and as they crawled through the intersection, they got to see the vehicles and debris and people up close.

Marquette was horrified. As she was telling me about it later, she was still stunned by what she had witnessed. Then she paused, reflecting on the morning, and said, "You know, Dad, I don't know why I was so annoyed. I couldn't find what I was looking for this morning, but something told me I just had to have it for school today." She shuddered, still remembering the crash scene. "But when I saw that accident, I just knew that if I had not needed it, that crash would have happened to us."

I didn't doubt it. I know my daughter has a strong intuition with things, just like I do. And there are hundreds of stories of people having very strong feelings to do, or not do, something which ended up saving their lives. Call it premonition, precognition, or coincidence…I was beginning to understand my daughter would be experiencing these events often in her life, as they just keep coming. Something within her seems to be tuned into the precise moments in time when she has to be diverted. All we had to do as parents is teach her to keep listening to those urges.

It's something we are navigating together as a family, but my wife and I never discounted her feelings or thoughts about stuff, as every time she thought we needed to veer off the intended path, or wait, or whatever, we have avoided something terrible happening. As she grows older, it becomes a more frequent phenomena. Whatever ESP or strong intuition she has inherited seems to be growing as she does.

Chapter Seven
SOCCER'S LIGHTNING

SCIENCE CAN EXPLAIN and prove a lot of things. I like to be able to have information about past and predicted future events when I am in a familiar or unfamiliar situation. Then it's just a matter of recalling that information when you need it. I am often amazed at how quickly our brains can pull out random information we didn't even realize we retained.

One of those times was when I was coaching my daughter's soccer team, which I did for a few years. One afternoon, as the game began, it was very warm with big, white clouds sprinkled across the sky. As in all kids' sports, some coaches and parents can be pretty irrational and ego driven when it comes to the games.

This particular afternoon, as soon as the game started, we scored two goals one after the other. I was proud of the girls. They had worked hard on their drills at their recent practices, and I was happy they were seeing their practice pay off. The other team's coach was not happy, and we could see him pacing and wringing his hands, angrily yelling commands at his team from the other sideline. I always feel bad for the kids when I see other coaches taking the game personally. It usually means most of the fun has left the game for their team.

In the distance, I could see bigger, darker clouds gathering, taking on the color of a deep bruise.

The other team scored a goal, and the score was now 2–1. They were gaining momentum. Their coach was even more animated and running along the sideline with the game, still yelling commands.

There was a distinctive crack and rumble from the wall of clouds and it started raining a little.

We scored one more goal. 3–1. The other coach started yelling louder. They scored a goal too, making it 3–2. It started hailing then, and with the sun still shining through a small gap in the dark, ominous clouds, it cast a surreal, dirty-orange light making the hailstones look like small, bright gem stones.

I motioned to get the referee's attention.

"Are you going to call the game?" I asked, knowing full well, as did the other coach, that he should be calling the game.

The rule book is very clear about clearing the field during any lightning storm or severe weather. It is called the 30-30 rule, where if you see lightning, you start counting, and if thunder is heard within 30 seconds, the game or practice is suspended for 30 minutes.

The other coach heard my question and yelled, frustrated, "It's just a little hail. Keep going. It's almost halftime anyway."

No sooner had he spoken the words than the hail got heavier and the girls started running from the field. The ref called halftime.

When halftime was coming to an end, the girls were getting ready to take the field. We were talking about strategy as I was bagging the balls. They were lined up side by side at the edge of the field getting ready to run on. One of them asked who was starting, and as I turned to answer, I saw that the girls all looked as if they were at the bottom of a deep swimming pool, their hair waving upwards as if underwater, shining with static electricity. I was horrified as time slowed down. I remembered with a jolt a program I had seen on the weather channel a couple of weeks before: if your hair is trying to touch the sky, you are in danger! Lightning was about to strike us!

I yelled at the girls to run, and as they took off sprinting, I looked over at the referee. I don't know if he heard me, but he was watching us with a goofy mid-chuckle look on his face. I thought he looked like the actor Don Knotts. He said, "The game is done," while motioning time and waving his arms as he was taking steps backwards, then stumbling as he turned and launched into an old man sprint to find cover.

The other coach ignored us all and kept his girls out on the field practicing. I figured he either didn't hear us, didn't believe us, didn't notice, or didn't care. It's always disappointing, though, watching another human so wrapped up in their own self-serving goals that they put other people's kids at risk. I would like to say it was the first time I had witnessed such arrogance, but it was not. And I knew it would not be the last time either.

We were lucky that day. We did not have to experience the horror of being on a field struck by lightning; just some heavy hail. Not that the other coach was any help. As if straight-up bluff and bluster can alter the weather. Although I would like to put those types of people in their place, I realize there is no point.

That's how sideline brawls get started, and then everyone looks like idiots.

But I was surprised by how clearly I had recalled the program I had watched about lightning and lightning strikes. I was surprised that I even remembered the bit about a person's hair reaching for the sky that meant imminent danger. It was just another program on TV. I didn't think I took that much notice. Apparently I did.

Which leads directly back to the one percent. There is a popular belief that we retain everything we see, hear, feel, and learn, way down deep in our subconscious. We just can't access all that knowledge at will.

So what makes us recall seemingly inconsequential pieces of information that are vital to a situation we are suddenly facing or about to face? Almost like we are being equipped before we need the information; a precognition even? There is no scientific evidence that precognition is real and is widely considered pseudoscience. Sure that looks good on paper, but talk to anyone who's experienced total recall in a situation and seeing it through the lens of precognition. I think you'd be hard pushed to say it was not real.

∞

So what did my daughter make of all these "events"? Curious like me? Full of wonder?

Nope; the total opposite. She hated that it happened, and was always more than ready to brush it off as a coincidence or not acknowledge it at all. When she was a kid, and then as a teen, we talked about almost everything. Marq and I have similar viewpoints, and we still do. My daughter is an amazing young woman. She comes from a long line of brave, intelligent, confident, and communicative women. She gets it from her mom's side as well, so there's not much she'll shy away from in conversation. Except this.

There are two separate events that happened to/with her that have her completely shook, and she is presently completely closed to even speculating or talking about her perceptiveness and how and why they might happen to her.

She calls them "bad energy" and doesn't even want to recall the details. I call them "premonitions" and think that they were good energy occurrences. Trusting her intuition and acting on it to find out she was right does not seem like bad energy to me. But as we all know, you can't tell your kids what to think. You can only offer your perspective and let them come to their own comfortable conclusions.

I think the events that she was an unwilling participant in are super interesting and prove without a doubt that she is predisposed to be sensitive to the one percent, hard-to-define events that happen around her. Why else would she wake up in the middle of the night to search for a loved one when she had no reason to think that anything was wrong? Just wide awake out of a deep sleep with a compulsive impulse to search for them, and then find them in crisis, alone.

I can only speculate that maybe it's because these events scared her, and she may have a little post-traumatic stress mixed with dread, but I think it's mainly because it does not fit comfortably into her own realm of present understanding about the universe and her place in it. So she doesn't want to think about it at all.

And I get it. She's a young adult now, starting to get comfortable in her chosen career, and is at a completely different point in her life. I imagine as she lives longer and develops curiosity for these things she may revisit them and ask questions about our lineage.

But then again, she may not.

All I know is that right now, at this point in our lives, she is not interested, and has made it very clear to her mother and I that they are her stories and we are not to bother her about them ever again.

So, that's that. For now anyway.

Chapter Eight
THE BIRDS

THERE ARE SOME things science still can't figure out. For example, medical science has a solid understanding about what causes people to go into a coma, and sometimes they will even induce a coma to prevent the body and brain from shutting down and ending life in extreme cases. But there is not an accurate picture of what causes a person to wake up from one, why sometimes a person will just wake up after a few days or weeks, months, or even years. And it's still impossible to predict whether a person will eventually recover, how long the coma will last, or if they'll have any long-term issues afterwards.

My sister Tanya went into a coma after an unexpected medical event, and about one week after that happened, I was at work one late afternoon. I'm a conductor on the railroad and have been for over thirty years. Because I coordinate and communicate with engineers and yardmasters about freight and passenger routes, I work a variety of conductor positions during the week. That day, I was working as a utility conductor, which is ground support for the trains getting in and out of the tracks.

It was a balmy, mid-seventies late summer afternoon and I was in T6 (Terminal 6) at Portland, Oregon's port dock. It was a very quiet afternoon when I got there in the utility vehicle. There was not a single soul around; no people at the waterfront Turtle Park just across the tracks; nobody paddling on the bay; no transients or homeless people on the benches; nobody. Which was rare, but just the way I liked it. I was parked at the very end of the dead end street, right by the stairs on the embankment that accessed the rail storage yard, awaiting instruction from the T6 yardmaster.

After awhile, he radioed to let me know the Z-Chicago-Portland train was coming in and the tracks needed to be lined for the storage six track. I had about twenty minutes.

"OK," I replied and immediately headed up the stairs to cross the yard and change the switches for the tracks. I started at number one and worked my way down the yard, aligning the switches for the incoming arrival. As I walked a little further and checked that they were aligned properly, I noticed a bird to the right of the track just standing there watching me. It was a small, black bird with orange at the tops of its wings like shoulder pads, and it was about five feet away from me. Having walked this track hundreds of times without being stared at by a bird, I stopped to look at it and we stood there staring at each other. It felt like this bird was staring into my soul.

Then, in a flash of chaos, it shot at me like an arrow, a blur of black and orange. I started swinging my hands wildly, suddenly filled with adrenaline, trying to comprehend what was happening. I dodged it frantically, and suddenly there was another one, and then three more, a nightmare-ish flurry of high-pitched squeaking and chirping and erratic wingbeats aiming at my face.

I spun around and took off running while trying to pick up gravel and rocks to throw at the birds which were now lining up and taking turns darting and dive-bombing at me. I twisted back around as I ran and almost fell a couple of times as I tried to turn to throw the rocks at them, which they all dodged, and I remember thinking how weird it was that they were executing a planned attack. Really...what the hell? I couldn't understand where they had come from or why. I also noticed they were not actually attacking or even touching me, more like playing a terrifying game of chicken, swooping in at high speed toward my face and swerving away at the last second, making way for the next one, squawking and screeching like they were trying to communicate something urgently to me.

I made it to the stairs without looking back or falling, and only paused to look back as the sound of high-pitched squawking and wings flapping was suddenly gone. I was breathing heavily in a panic. I could feel my heart pounding in my chest, and I was confused, desperately glancing behind me to see if they were just repositioning for another attack.

They were nowhere in sight. Five aggressive birds, who just dived and bombarded me for an unnerving sprint through the yard, had vanished. That was even more spooky than the unexpected attack. The sudden silence made me question my mental health.

Right then my phone rang. As I answered it, I was still on high alert, expecting the birds to appear and start diving at me again. It was my brother Ronny letting me know that they had turned off the machines keeping Tanya alive and that she had passed away. I was winded and trying to control my breathing so he wouldn't hear me panting.

Then he wanted to make plans for us to drive down to Compton, California with our other brothers for the funeral. I was still panting from fright as I was trying to speak, and Ronny heard me. He asked if I was OK, thinking I was upset about Tanya's untimely passing. Not wanting to tell him about what just happened with the birds, I told him I was fine. He suggested we talk about it later. I agreed and ended the call.

As I bent over to prop myself on my knees and take a couple of deep breaths to get control of myself again, the birds flew overhead in a perfect inverted V formation like military jets do at ceremonies. I stood up and watched them fly off into the distance. I knew they had something to do with my sister's passing. I knew that's what they were trying to communicate. All I could say with a nervous laugh was, "Damn you, Tanya."

It has long been accepted in alternative thinking communities that birds are symbolic of loved ones letting us know they are around when they have passed. Blackbirds in particular, like the red-winged blackbirds that visited me, have long been associated with death.

Tanya was probably the smartest one in our family, naturally talented, and never had to study. When she was in high school she could read a book once on something and then ace the test. She got her nursing degree in her late forties and did that from scratch. A queen mastering being a queen of all trades? Maybe.

I couldn't help but think that when the plug was pulled and she was moving on from this earthly plane that she took a detour before moving on.

A little while later, I had a total memory recall about when she came to visit for a couple of weeks in my youth, and almost every night she would open a bottle of wine and sit and listen to the record player playing her favorite song over and over for hours…it was Bob Marley's "Three Little Birds."

> "Rise up this morning, smiled with the rising sun
> Three little birds pitch by my doorstep
> Singing sweet songs of melodies pure and true
> Saying, 'This is my message to you-ou-ou.'
>
> Singing, 'Don't worry about a thing
> 'Cause every little thing is gonna be all right.'"

Remembering that shook me to my core. I felt a deep connection to the supernatural and my sister when I put all these events together.

Another case for the one percent—scientifically unable to be recreated—but anyone who has ever experienced a visitation by a bird or birds from a recently passed loved one knows there is so much more to communication with the other side than is commonly accepted.

Chapter Nine
THE ANSWER

After Tanya's funeral, I was feeling unbalanced and weary. The coincidental events had a mind-bending effect and were messing with my head. I was trying to explain them to myself; to make it fit. It was like I had pieces to a puzzle but didn't know what the picture was supposed to be, or if I even had all the pieces. I was also looking for answers that made sense about Tanya and her birds, half wondering if it was going to happen again.

I thought I could discuss these things with various trusted friends and shared a little bit here and there to see their receptivity. Well, they were not receptive and definitely not interested in anything weird or unusual that I wanted to share. So I stopped trying to tell them. I was having enough difficulty figuring it out on my own without their doubt. Was it all just a coincidence?

I have heard people say they don't believe in coincidences,

that it is the hand of God or Divine Presence in every "coincidental" moment. I can see the logic in that. It makes sense that due to the very nature of seemingly random events often leading to, or being the catalyst for redirection in people's lives, no matter how seemingly inconsequential at the time, it often feels like a higher power, or intelligence, is in the background orchestrating such things.

At the funeral, I got to talking to one of my sisters, Carolyn, and I asked her if it was possible for my daughter and I to have the same dreams at the same time.

Carolyn is highly educated, with a PhD in Education and a published dissertation to her credit. She has an open, scientific mind, is very intelligent, and was receptive to the conversation. I don't know why I hadn't thought about asking her before.

As predicted, she gave me a very scientific reply, that humans are evolving and continue to evolve generation over generation, and the idea that humans can communicate without words and through energy alone is a very real possibility. Another sister, Diana, joined the conversation and added that humans do not know all there is to know and definitely do not know all the information that the universe holds (that one percent). We also touched on shared dreaming. This made sense to me too.

My relationship with my sister Carolyn was not a stereotypical brother/sister relationship. She was much older than me. As the first of the eleven kids my mom and dad had together, but number five of the fifteen total, she has an incredible capacity for grit and getting stuff done. With a PhD in Education, she was raised in Compton, California and put her ex through college, paid and everything, all through her own hard work. She is highly intelligent and we can talk for hours about anything and everything—with or without cocktails. Heh.

I would see her at different family functions here and there, and I stayed with her a few times. It was cool to see we have very similar habits and behaviors, right down to the way we associate people with their politics, our eating habits, and our thought processes.

She is one of the most put together, professional people I know. Well, until you tick her off, and that Compton survival sass kicks in. That side IS NOT pretty.

One time, wheeling her through airport security, they would not allow her to take her yogurt on the plane.

"You can take it if it's frozen," she snapped. Security said it wasn't frozen. She said it was.

I had to keep moving through to the search area, waiting for her. She was about twenty feet away from me in her wheelchair, and I could hear her cussing and sassing the TSA officers from there. I was just waiting for them to come and get me and kick us both out of the airport, or send us to jail or something as they found more things to be debated. Luckily that did not happen that day.

Another famous story in our family is when Carolyn was a kid at the table at dinnertime and she and Kathy got into a squabble about something. Carolyn was so mad she threw a fork across the table and it stabbed Kathy in the hand like a dart. Our family has many tales from the dinner table that rival that one. With so many personalities, there was always a beef somewhere.

Carolyn reminds me of a character in a movie, the one who was sent to investigate the protagonist and do it with such drive and determination, she would find the one thing that would reveal the truth of a situation.

I consider Carolyn the Second Oracle under Mom, and she is my big-sis-besty. I can ask her anything, and if she doesn't know the answer (although she usually does), she will research the topic to get the best answer for me.

She put my mind at ease after listening to everything I told her about all the events I had experienced just by the fact that she believed me and validated my experiences. She is definitely in the top two of opinions and perspectives I respect, with God or the Creator being number one. I don't yet know that entity, but as you can see, I'm working on it.

I think there are no such things as coincidences, and that these events are actually mislabeled synchronicities, two events that come together for a purpose, whether it's to give us a message, or to move life in a different direction. Often, however, the message is only available if you are paying attention. I decided I needed to start paying better attention.

Chapter Ten
DEATH CHRONICLES

I FIND THE LONGER I live and the more I experience, the more I notice how much grief, guilt, and uncertainty is wrapped in religion and life in general. How people process and deal with death is often a surprise; everyone has their own way of doing it, and nobody is wrong.

I like to think that people arrive at their own beliefs through their individual journeys in life. None of us are perfect. With that being said, people are going to do what people want to do and you usually can't stop them.

You probably think your ideas and beliefs are the best and right ones, for you anyway. And you can lead a horse to water, but you can't make it drink. I tell my wife this all the time.

I do know one thing though: it is usually a very good idea to stay in contact with loved ones—even if it is just a quick chat, text message, card, or whatever. You never know when you are providing a life line, for them, or yourself.

My sister Diana converted to Islam years ago and changed her name to Habeeba. She was such a free spirit; nobody was surprised when she found another belief system that fit her thought processes. She lived with us for a short time when I was in junior high and was always counseling me on the power of formal education, even though we didn't have all the answers to life's mysteries, and probably never would. She also taught me how to drive her Cadillac Eldorado. She was very good-natured and always cheerful and upbeat. Her conversations were interesting and to the point. I liked having her around.

Years earlier, when I was about seven, she had sent her daughter Consuella—Connie for short—to stay with me and my mom. It was one of the best times of my childhood and stands out like a glowing beacon of childhood bliss when I remember that late summer and fall. We had such a great time and did everything together: swam, ran around outside, played all sorts of games, made up stories, stayed up late, and watched TV together. We loved all the same characters and shows.

Having Connie with us was the most amazing thing that had happened to me up until then. It was like having a best-friend sister 24/7. I secretly hoped she would stay with us forever.

After around four months, though, Connie really wanted to go home. She missed her mom, Habeeba, so Mom sent her back. I missed her for a long time; my best friend and running buddy had gone. The house was quieter and things were kind of dull.

The following summer, almost nine months after she had left, I was swimming at the public pool one afternoon and my mom came to get me. She looked concerned as she came over and said,

"Donny, get out. We have to go." My mom is the only one that called me Donny, and I got out of the pool right away wondering what was wrong. She didn't even say hello or anything, just commanded me to get out of the pool. I wondered if I was in trouble. As I was wrapping my towel around me, she blurted out, "Connie is dead." I thought she said something else, not wanting to believe what I just heard. "Huh?"

As we were heading outside, she said it again, "Connie is dead. It probably happened shortly after we sent her back home." She had big tears running down her face, but her voice never changed. I struggled to understand what she was telling me. I felt like I had cotton wool in my throat and I couldn't swallow properly, so I did my best to keep up with her through the parking lot as she was striding ahead of me.

What I remember most from the conversation is that she never said "missing." How could she have known Connie was dead without having all the details? I didn't have any doubt; she just knew.

Habeeba had just gotten too far away from the family and was so distant.

Nobody was ever charged with Connie's murder, and they never found her body. Nobody served time for taking her life away. There was an unspoken assumption that Habeeba's longtime boyfriend had something to do with it. Mom later admitted she thought Habeeba had met the wrong guy, but she respected her daughter's choice. But it changed our entire family's lives forever.

Like so many families, there are pockets of intense grief and unresolved trauma in our family, and some people were extremely unforgiving concerning this event. I can't say I blame them. I was just a kid, so obviously I was not privileged to the conversations or actions taken concerning Connie's disappearance. I was aware of grief like a heavy wet blanket covering us. It was there for a long time. I don't know why I never thought to ask my mom about it before she passed.

My mom's grief was with her for the rest of her life, but she did not let that stop her from moving forward with her own life's journey. It was always there though. Right up until her death, she would spontaneously cry bitterly when she'd get triggered, and I knew what she was thinking—if she had not sent her grandchild back, or if she'd just kept her for a little longer, if she'd told Connie it was for the best that she stayed with us, or told Habeeba that she should come and visit her daughter, just kept Connie for an extra few weeks, or another few months, or even the whole year, there would have been a different result and Connie would still be with us. I felt exactly the same way. I know I was only seven or eight, but kids take on a lot of guilt for things they have no control over.

My mother knew we all make mistakes in life—heaven knows I do it on a daily basis—but I think it's how you deal with those mistakes that is the real key to succeeding in life. Or at least getting through the time that we are here.

I remember years later, after Tanya's funeral, Habeeba sent me a message via social media telling me how handsome I looked with my dreads. I was surprised and flattered. We had very little contact for many years until then, and I understood she had been sick with one thing or another and recovered, but I had no idea what was going on with her.

I was too busy living my own life. I started thinking about her, though, and I now know I should have called her and at least had a quick conversation, said hello or something, but I did not.

Again, I missed the proverbial boat.

I declined the opportunity to visit her shortly after as well. Other family members went to see her in California and came back saying she was OK, so I thought all was well with her. I should have reached out, but I didn't.

Turned out, all was not well with her.

Habeeba died a few days later. I was shocked.

Immediately I thought I should have had a conversation with her years ago, you know, three Hennessey's and a can of whoop ass.

It turned out my sister had Hepatitis C, and for whatever reason, she refused medical treatment after being diagnosed.

She did not want to take a simple course of antibiotics to kill off a virus.

Was it because of her religion? It's hard to tell what her logic was. She thought the virus could be treated by naturopathic and herbal treatments. Habeeba didn't recover and ended up with some serious liver damage, ultimately resulting in complete liver failure.

In conjunction with the other health challenges she was facing, which all seemed to compound one another at exactly the same time, she was admitted to hospital and flatlined, coded blue for a minute or two, until they brought her back.

She wasn't expected to recover then, but she did.

Kidney failure was then added to her long list of growing ailments and she was on regular dialysis, but due to her liver failure, she was not a candidate for a kidney transplant. It seemed she eventually succumbed to the combination of medical issues she had.

I wish I had more contact with her, although I realize she may not have given a thought to my voice of reason, but I didn't give myself a chance to even try. It still sticks with me, and her death resonated with me deeply. I felt I could have provided the game-changing perspective for her. Maybe I'm a control freak; who knows.

Shoulda, coulda, woulda, right?

Grief pushes me to do better things and not dwell on it. Regardless of her imperfections, I loved her. I know she loved me for all of mine too.

Rest in peace, Habeeba. You were loved. I know you did your best.

Chapter Eleven
JUST MISSED IT

One bonus of being the baby of a large family was that lots of my nieces and nephews were not too much older or younger than me. From early childhood until we were adults, we used to have a blast together. I was close to my niece Nichole being that we were only a few years apart in age. She was always up for doing something and had such a vibrant personality. There was never a dull moment when we hung out. She could also be a little rough around the edges at times, especially if she felt disrespected. But all my nieces are like that, so I guess that's just a family trait. Strong women are everywhere in my family.

She lived in Houston and I went to visit her only once as an adult. It was a short trip, but it was so good to see her and see she was doing very well for herself. Then a couple of years passed and I had not seen or talked to her; you know how life just gets busy.

Then I started seeing her beautiful photo pop up on social media a lot. In fact, it was so often, she started weighing on my mind and I thought I should reach out and see how she was. I even told my wife that I had been thinking about Nichole and I should contact her. Kim agreed and told me if I kept thinking about her, I should just go. I promised myself I would get around to at least calling her, but I am a world-class procrastinator and I never did.

Then one day, about a month after I told my wife I should go see Nichole, one of my siblings called to let me know Nichole had unexpectedly passed away. Her daughter walked into the kitchen one morning and found her on the floor dead.

Come to find out, she had been experiencing severe headaches and was taking over-the-counter medication for them which wasn't working. She didn't go to the doctor because she didn't think she needed to. We discovered she had untreated hypertension. The high blood pressure had been causing the headaches, but she didn't know she had high blood pressure, so obviously she was not taking care of it. The unchecked blood pressure caused a spike in pressure in her brain which caused a massive stroke along with damage to her other organs. It would have been an intense but fairly instant death.

Another sister called me, a little after the funeral, and said, "You know, I'm just wondering about this whole life thing." And I knew what she meant. I was still incredulous that I didn't follow my gut, even though I had multiple urges to call and go see her. She was on my mind for almost four months. I didn't do anything and she died as a result. Or so I told myself.

I have flashbacks to when we were younger and I would visit her often in Portland. We would sit and talk about everything. I used to notice then that sometimes, when we were talking, she would squint and her eyes would partially roll back in her head, or she would flinch and roll her eyes to the side like there was something in one of them, but there never was. I could never figure out if she was just giving me sass or something else was going on with her. I wonder now if those were signs of high blood pressure or another issue that had gone undiagnosed. I wonder if I could have changed her outcome, helped her somehow. I can't help but feel if I had gone to see her, we would have had a few cocktails and I could have made her see sense and get to a doctor. I've had family tell me there was nothing I could have done, but I'm not so sure.

On some level, I knew that something was up with her, and I didn't listen to myself. I didn't do anything about it. Not even a phone call.

I had a heavy heart for a long time after that. I truly regret not contacting her or listening to my gut.

I think that we know some people so well we can automatically detect small changes in their energy and would often be able to help or offer perspective if we just took ourselves seriously enough to follow up on our instincts, to listen to that quiet inner voice.

But life is too busy. We don't have enough time. There is too much other noise, too many emergencies to deal with right in front of us. We always think we have tomorrow. We don't take ourselves seriously enough to pay attention, or maybe we just misinterpret the whole thing. It's hard to say.

I am working on being able to pay attention to the quiet voice and act on those nudges to reach out more often, but it's a constant struggle. Does the fact that we are all able to pick up on energy around us all the time, yet never act on it, fall into the one percent?

Or does the part about having intuition about someone else's death make it the one percent?

Once again, I feel like I just missed it.

Chapter Twelve
ON MY MIND

I WAS BEGINNING TO take notice of the people that kept entering my thoughts when it came to untimely passings. This seemed to be another of those mysterious synchronicities that continually lined up and I was paying more attention to. I also noticed I was still resistant, however, and it often took me awhile to make the connection.

Another one I thought of often was KJ. He was like blood to me growing up. We had a solid bond. I was also real close with his mom and grandmother. I was at his house a lot as a teenager and his grandmother and I shared a close bond too. She was like a second mother to me, a mentor, favorite aunt, and older sister all rolled into one. KJ kept popping up on my social media feed as "people you may know," and, after deleting the suggestion multiple times—after all I was usually just on social media to find information about an event or see something my wife posted—I started to question why it kept popping up over and over, and started wondering how KJ was and what he was doing.

KJ was always such a cool cat, and I had not seen him in such a long time. I even got to thinking it would be good to see him. But I told myself it wasn't that important, so I didn't put much effort into actually doing anything about it. If I'm honest, though, I did feel a constant underlying curiosity. I needed to see him. Where was he at? And what was he doing? How was his life? Was it going well for him? How were his mom and grandmother? These questions kept returning. I still didn't do anything about it besides THINK I should do something.

And then, it was too late. Again.

Out of the blue, one of his family members called me to let me know he had passed away. He was diagnosed with a blood disease and died suddenly. I felt bad that I hadn't reached out. Next shock was his mom dying a week or so later. I never found out what ended her life, but suffice it to say, I imagined she died of a broken heart, her boy struck down and gone within a few months. Then, only a couple of weeks after that, the grandmother died too. I found out she had asked about me a few months before she passed, right around the time I had been thinking I should contact KJ.

Nobody told me until it was too late, obviously. I probably would have made more of an effort to get in touch if I'd heard KJ's grandmother was asking after me too. We had shared an almost spiritual bond when I was younger. I felt very close to her. We just got each other. We used to see things the same way, and she was a great lady.

But that didn't happen. And I can't help but wonder if I'd really missed anything. I never got the chance to catch up with all three of them before they passed. Never got that chance for a final chat with any of them. It was a bummer, but I wasn't devastated or anything. It was just missing someone. That strange, empty feeling of knowing they are no longer there. Just gone. What could have I done anyway? Nothing I would have been able to do or say would have changed their outcome. I still missed them though.

Once again, I was late on my impulse to reach out to someone I was thinking of, like my sister Habeeba, or my niece Nichole. I told myself that if it happened again, I would definitely make a better effort to contact these people. Or at least would try. Or I told myself I would.

I still didn't fully understand the impulse or push from within to contact people I randomly thought of. Was it precognition? Or just missing people from my past that somehow I picked up that they were not long for this world? Which would make it precognition, right?

Except it didn't happen in dreams. It was more of a feeling (which I often did not act on quickly enough), and did I really think that by reaching out to these people I would somehow delay their untimely passing? Or was it just a nudge to reconnect with people who had meant a lot to me in the past?

I don't know. I have learned from this (amongst other things) that regret is powerful and I hoped to avoid that feeling again.

Chapter Thirteen
NOT KATHY?!

THE FEELING OF heaviness was lingering. I found ignoring the nudges about visiting or calling people, who then unexpectedly passed away, was a weight I could not shake because I knew it was not coincidental, and I had ignored my gut and missed the synchronicities. I was about done with death by that point. But, of course, you are never "about done" with death.

The day my social media feed suggested a connection with my sister Kathy, I was shocked. She barely ever used social media, and this was not a coincidence.

I knew I had to go see her. I didn't even question it or put it off. Not Kathy!

Kathy is one of my older sisters—twenty two years older than me, in fact. She was the mother for so many when Mom wasn't available, and is one of the sweetest, most loving people on this earth. She took care of everyone, from the cradle all the way to the grave for a few too. Her spirit is vibrant, and she glows from within, which makes you feel warm inside just from being around her.

If there was a dictionary meaning of my sister Kathy, it would say: Compton's Betty Crocker and Greatest Homemaker.

Selfless is her fame and unconditional love is her game.

I called her to let her know I was coming and booked the trip that afternoon.

I spent the flight to see her, recalling the fondest memories of when I'd go to California as a kid to stay with her in the house she'd lived in forever. There was never a dull moment; we'd go to Knott's Berry Farm, Disneyland, drive-in movies, you name it. It was always a blast. I loved being there in my youth.

She was so welcoming and accepting of everyone that her house was the family meeting place for a lot of family gatherings and family functions through the years. It was always the natural choice.

When I knocked at the door and saw her beautiful face light up with the biggest smile, an immediate sense of relief washed over me, taking away all the heavy thoughts and filling me with ease, happiness, and well being. I could only spend one full day with her, but it was well worth it, and it warmed my heart to see how well she was doing.

Hers is the sort of love that leaves you feeling supported and cherished.

My sister's expertise is love: pure, unconditional, and real. If not for her impact and love, so many family members would have failed for sure. She is a true queen in every sense of the word. Hail, hail to Compton's true queen.

I realized then that maybe the nudges from within aren't

always about people dying. Sometimes they are about spending time with the people that are just good for your heart and soul, the people that fill you up with love and give you the strength to cope with whatever is coming down the line at you. Maybe our bodies are more in tune with the universe and our connection to God, Buddha, the universe, or whichever higher power you believe in, than we give them credit for. I don't know for sure, but seeing Kathy and basking in the unconditional love of a big sister refilled my cup and gave me the strength to endure the events that were still looming on the horizon.

Science recognizes love with various studies being conducted over the last two decades on the effects love has on a person. It has been proven that high quality social and familial relationships can reduce stress, and I'd believe it. I think if every family had a member like Kathy, the world would be a much healthier place.

I think love makes up a huge portion of the one percent. Maybe love is the very origin of the entire one percent?

Hard to say.

Chapter Fourteen
LAS VEGAS

ALCOHOL AND I HAVE had a twisted relationship over the years. I've relied heavily on its ability to always be there, ready to take my overthinking away. Although it often took it away so swiftly it was like I became another person. There were two versions of me. There was my Dr. Jeykll version—everyone's favorite Uncle-Dante-the-Great-Cancer-Empath—and then there was my Mr. Hyde who showed up in my grayed- or blacked-out drinking episodes. I've seen video evidence of that one, and let's just say, he ain't classy or pretty.

But this love/hate relationship, without realizing it until later, has often blessed me with the right person at the right time: family, friends, co-workers, supervisors, judges, lawyers, law enforcement, bartenders, bouncers, and my wife who have all swooped in at the exact right moment and saved me from utter destruction. It got to the point where I just had to tell people,

"If you have a problem with the drunk version of me, don't take it up with the sober me, please, 'cause I have no clue." Not proud of that, but I'm just being honest.

Funny how we seem to devolve into disregard for ourselves at different times, and things are so much clearer upon reflection.

I could never figure out why, though, yet I have always believed you cannot save somebody from themselves. But then, thinking about my own drunk, crazy character metamorphosis, as well as the people I've been blessed with and when, I think there is a chance I might be wrong.

That being said, alcohol has also done me some favors over the years. Going to a casino and impulsively putting a five-dollar chip on double sixes and winning over $500 on my first bet at a craps table is a good memory. Similar events happened often. I would not have been so impulsive if it hadn't been for alcohol. And there have been a few times when Dr. Jekyll has firmly stepped back in and taken control, like when I remembered I had coaching with Marquette the next day. So the very nature of my drunken switch between the two is curious. It's almost like the grayed-out drunk me is still able to be pulled back under control by Dr. Jekyll, whereas the blacked-out drunk me is very definitely taken over by Mr. Hyde.

And then there is when alcohol ends up doing me a favor in the long run, but not so much in the short term.

One night I had stopped by my nephew Dantrell's house after having a few drinks, buzzed, and on my way to the Mr. Hyde version of me. It wasn't too late and I was feeling all peace and love, Uncle-Dante-the-Great-Cancer-Empath, and I gave my grand nephew and niece some money, cuz, let's face it, cash is better than candy to kids. I was sitting there talking to them, and we were all having a great time laughing and talking smack about a sports team, and apparently I said a couple of curse words—I blame Mr. Hyde for that one; I don't usually drop curses in everyday conversation—and I honestly hadn't even realized I did it. We were just shooting the breeze.

But Dantrell's wife overheard and took exception to it, so she told Dantrell to "deal with me," which he did by calling me into his room and chastising me like a kid, and then rounded it out with the new rule that I wasn't to come over unless I called first. This was basically unheard of till then. We were always just stopping in as we went by; no problem. No one in my family ever called each other in the same city to say we were coming over. We all just show up. If we have to travel, that's different. But across town, that was always "door's always open!"

I was really embarrassed, and Dr. Jekyll slunk out the door immediately.

Well, months went by, and as life had it, I didn't see Dantrell or his wife and kids at all during that time. Whenever I thought I'd stop by, I'd feel embarrassed still and would forget to call until I was right outside their house, which I figured they wouldn't like either, so I never went.

When he posted on social media about celebrating his birthday the first weekend of October, in Las Vegas, I had a moment of thinking how great it would be to take Kim and Marq for a family trip to Vegas and join him for it. Kim and I talked about it, but I felt weird. I couldn't pinpoint if it was the lingering embarrassment and the fact that we hadn't hung out since that happened, or something else.

It would be a good trip for us, I rationalized. Marquette and Kim love to be real tourists whenever we go anywhere and would happily be out and about all day, visiting all the tourist destinations, shopping, and soaking it all in. Whereas I'm the opposite.

My favorite place to investigate in a new city is the local sports bar, with a few quiet drinks, and some big screen TVs, maybe place a few bets. Vegas has some great sports bars. There would be enough to amuse us all.

There was also a huge country music festival that was going to be right on the strip. It did sound like a fun weekend. Marq and Kim are big music fans and listen to all genres of music. Kim said she'd like to take Marquette for the closing night on Sunday if we decided to go.

I wasn't feeling it though. Besides, with my wounded pride and lingering embarrassment, I didn't feel the same excited "Vegas Baby!" energy as I had from previous trips. I told my wife I'd think about it, and she was fine either way.

That music festival did look like it would be worth seeing. It was an annual event and was held right on the strip at the Las Vegas village. I considered it for a couple of weeks, going back and forth between just swallowing my embarrassment and joining my nephew, family, and friends to party for a weekend and get out of town with Marquette and Kim, or listening to my gut feeling that I just didn't want to go.

Much in all as I loved going to Vegas, the energy around even the thought of going this time was still "off." I couldn't convince myself that we needed to make the trip. I decided to trust my gut and decline. That was my last thought about it and I put it out of my head. We could catch up with Dantrell and his family before they went or when they got back. No biggie.

I told myself it was because I was still embarrassed, but a month or so later, on the weekend of his birthday celebration in Las Vegas, that theory was blown out of the water when on Sunday, October 1st, I turned on the news and felt all the breath sucked out of me in an instant. It was the breaking news story about a gunman firing into the crowd of 22,000 people at the festival from the 32nd floor of the Mandalay Bay Hotel, diagonally across from the Vegas Village festival area.

A single shooter fired over 1,000 shots into the crowd for over 15 minutes, killing 58 people at the event and injuring over 800. I could not believe what I was seeing. The relief that washed over me was palpable. I was so glad I had listened to those gut feelings, whatever they truly were—lingering embarrassment, or a nudge from the universe telling me to not take my family to Las Vegas that weekend.

Thankfully, none of our friends or family that went to Las Vegas went to the festival as they aren't big country fans. They did get caught up in the frantic craziness of trying to leave the next day though.

I talked to Kim about it, and she was stunned too. She didn't want to think about what could have happened if they had gone to the festival that Sunday evening.

She plays Bonko once a month with a bunch of her friends, and after the next game, she came home with some surreal stories of the people some of them knew that had been at the concert.

Even hearing it secondhand from Kim, I got goosebumps. A daughter of one of the employees of the school district went with some friends. They were all separated in the sheer chaos and horror that ensued. The girl managed to fly home to Portland without ID. Lucky her dad has connections. Her friends got home OK too. And there was another story of someone who survived that event only to be shot and killed a few weeks later in another shooting. The stories were harrowing and made me think of what hell those people had been through. I couldn't even start to imagine the scene as it played out.

In light of everything, I know it was not the embarrassment of the situation all those months ago that created my apprehension about going.

I spoke with Dantrell about the drinking incident a little while after this happened, and he said he'd been thinking that he should have handled it differently. I don't. I think it all played out exactly as it was supposed to. I'm not big on coincidence.

Mostly I felt personally satisfied that I had listened to my gut feeling for a change and followed my instinct.

Chapter Fifteen
THE MATRIARCH

MY MOTHER DIED in November of 2018, just three weeks before her 95th birthday. Her name was Eartha Lee Williams, and she was born in Louisiana in 1923. She graduated high school and married Daddy in the same year, at nineteen years old, welcoming his four children from his previous marriage as if they were her own. She and my dad had eleven kids together. It was a full house for sure.

Not long after they married in 1942, they moved from Louisiana to Southern California, seeking better opportunities for themselves, as the South was not the best place for a growing colored family in those days. Not a lot of opportunity or fair pay. There was still a lot going on that made parents worry for their children too.

Mom loved her family and was devoted to them all. She had a feisty and passionate spirit. She was strong-willed and determined. My mother was a true homemaker with exceptional cooking, sewing, and decorating skills. She was also well known in the community for her beautiful soprano singing voice.

My mom did not mess around and would not hesitate to set you straight or put you in your place and remind you she was your mother. She was Queen Bee.

But she looked out for all of her family and would always be there in times of need, often before you even knew you needed her. She was tuned in to her family.

When she died, there were eight surviving children, twenty-eight grandchildren, thirty-five great grandchildren and nine great great grandchildren. Since then, our family continues to grow, with more grandkids, great grandkids and even great great grandchildren entering the world. Together, there are enough of us to create a small town or an army battalion.

My mother also believed in education. She did not go to university herself, but she encouraged every single one of her children, and her children's children, to go to college.

As a result, we are a very educated family. There are a couple of doctors, many teachers, technicians, engineers, and a number of highly educated and skilled individuals in my family.

My mom always assured me that, as her last child, I was the best of the bunch, and the apple of her eye.

Sure, each child was wonderful in their own way, but no matter my accomplishments, or failures, she would always insist I was the cream of her crop. I was always like, "Sure, Mom, if you say so." I always felt a little embarrassed, but mostly proud, that she called me that.

There are stories about how some of the others would be laying in bed with Mom when I was a toddler and then as a little kid, and when I showed up for cuddle time she would kick them out of the bed. To this day some of my siblings are still resentful about that, like it was my fault, although it's a good-natured grudge. But then, I can't really tell sometimes. Heh!

Although her unwavering belief in me was empowering, she was blatant about me being the favorite, and it would wear on some of my other siblings, nieces, and nephews. As the last of my dad's fifteen children and my mom's eleven, I can understand that by the time I arrived I was probably the easiest, with my closest sibling already eight years older than me. The house was less chaotic and busy, and I was the baby of the family. I spent a lot of quality time with my mom, and we were very close. I was truly a mama's boy, and by the time I was ten, pretty much everyone was out of the house, and the couple that were still at home didn't want their little brother tagging along.

We had a tight bond, me and Mom, and I knew her on many levels my siblings did not. She taught me all sorts of things about things seen, and unseen, things felt and understood, about God and the afterlife. This was my introduction to the one percent and was just part of our lives. She took me everywhere with her and taught me how to make the floral arrangements she was so good at. I liked making them with her, but it wasn't a skill that I used much in life.

My mother was the matriarch of our large family. There was no question about her authority over all fifteen children, their spouses, and their own children, a figurehead much like the first Oracle from the Matrix movies. I was the equivalent of Neo, her apprentice and understudy. I know each one of her kids knew her on deep levels, but if you talk to them they all have different versions of our mother.

I had the version of Mom who thought I was the best, the cream of the crop. We had the same soul.

After I left home, she would often bench the other children and send a request for me especially to come and help her, even if I lived the furthest away. And of course I would go. Mom needed me. I was always available for her.

Later in her life, when she was living in Texas, she ended up in a nursing home. The details are harsh but irrelevant, some family feud or disruption, or some sort of big old mess in our family, which was not surprising in the least. So many people, so much love, and so many opinions mean there's always a drama somewhere. It was just part of our family dynamic, and I didn't know anything different.

Anyway, Mom was stuck in Texas in a nursing home, and three or four other family members had gone down to Texas to bring her back. But she was not having it. For whatever reason, she did not trust anybody. I didn't ask, because no doubt there were multiple versions of events.

Nobody could convince her to return with them to the Northwest. I spoke with some other family members, and I had questions. She did say, however, she would only return if I flew down to get her. Nothing they were saying made much sense, but I knew Mom was calling for her youngest boy, her blessed son, the cream of the crop, to come and get her.

I went without hesitation, and when I got to the nursing home, seeing her face light up, and all the life return to her eyes with the biggest smile I've ever seen on her face, made me feel like a little kid, her number one again. I took her back to Vancouver, Washington with me, and not long after, she ended up moving back to California and living with one of her granddaughters, which worked out well for everybody.

I would visit her and we would talk about everything, reminiscing about me growing up and the experiences we shared. We would talk into the wee small hours of the morning, and I would crash out in her bed, hoping she didn't talk in her sleep.

During my last visit with her, one morning when I woke up, I was looking around her room, and even though her bed was very close to the floor, I was thinking about a few people I knew who recently experienced their loved ones taking falls out of bed, and that maybe she needed some guardrails on her bed so it didn't happen to her. I thought maybe I should run it by my niece.

But as I lay there, playing the conversation out in my head, I realized it was futile. The conflict it would cause wouldn't be worth it, and then there'd be others to deal with too. The ladies in my family sure have sharp tongues—I think they'd even put the devil in his place. The menfolk in the family are kept firmly under control with their caustic comments and defenses. I could hear them already in my head, "You can't tell us what to do! You ain't here to take care of her!" "You mind your own business Dante." "Where you been for the last few years?" "Don't tell us what to do," etc...

In retrospect, I should have said something regardless. I should have taken them out for a few drinks and convinced them of what a good idea it would be, to stop Mom from falling out of bed. I should have just bought the rail for her bed and installed it myself.

One of my lesser-known talents is that, over a few drinks, I can convince anyone of anything. Geez, I could convince the pope to come to a gentleman's club with me.

But, as they say, hindsight is 20/20.

I thought about it a few more times after I flew back home, but decided to leave it alone. Almost seven months later, Mom fell out of bed and broke her hip. I wasn't surprised, but more disappointed in myself, that the cream of the crop didn't trust his instincts again, and pushed the matter with my niece. It's an awful feeling when I don't listen to my own messages to myself. Again.

I bought tickets for me and my wife, our daughter, and her boyfriend to go to California to see her as soon as we could. I impulsively also bought tickets back for a week after our return so we could get back to see another family member who wasn't there at the time. I had the very strong feeling we needed to see her, and besides, it would be good to check on Mom again.

Mom didn't know we were coming, and as we waited in the hospital cafeteria, it took a really long time for them to bring her out. I knew that wasn't a good sign. She had already undergone hip surgery to repair the break and was not doing well.

When they wheeled her out, she looked very small and like her legs were glued together. She got such a surprise she started crying when she saw us. She couldn't believe we had come all the way from Washington State to see her. It was a bittersweet moment. I was so glad we came, but it hurt my heart to see her. She didn't talk much, and she wasn't hungry. She was miserable and not really there. I wished she would die right then. I could feel all the physical and emotional pain she was in and that she had given up.

The nurse that was with her told us she had started rehabilitation that day, but I knew that wouldn't help her. She was already half gone.

We went back to her room with her as she had no appetite and didn't want to eat anything in the cafeteria. We hung out for a little while making small talk. We all told her how much we loved her and left. That was the last time I saw Mom. She died a few days later of sepsis created by intestinal problems.

The doctor said she wouldn't have survived a second surgery, as even a healthy young adult would have a long recovery from a second major surgery.

It turned out to be very synchronistic that I had bought those second tickets which we used to return for her funeral. Although I was glad I had paid attention to the synchronicities about going to see Mom that time, I felt guilty that I didn't buy the bed rail.

Was I finally listening to my instincts, or God, or the universe, or whatever it is that gives us the nudge, and tells us something? Or was it just because it was Mom?

I didn't cry at all leading up to, during, or after her funeral. I feel I had done all my grieving years before as we went through so many other tragic experiences together. She always taught me that death was just part of life's processes.

My mother was selfless. She was the sort of person who would completely understand if you'd have to miss a funeral for a big, important reason like meeting the president, or a final college exam, or a life-altering interview. The way she saw it was that she would rather you did that instead of going to a funeral and being sad. She ran her race and now expected everyone else to run theirs, not to waste it by sitting around moping.

Take it from the cream of the crop: she was loving, strong, and dedicated to her family and God. She was one of a kind, the epitome of the one percent, and I'm sure she's proud of her family and the legacy of love she left behind. Heh!

Chapter Sixteen

In Closing: The One Percent DNA/Omniscience/Unity Consciousness/Love

As far as I can understand, 99 percent of our awareness (the "our" I'm referring to is humanity as a generalized collective) is taken up by our daily lives, the things we must do to survive, and the mindset we must retain to fit into society. The 99 percent is SIMPLE LOGIC.

We have enough awareness to harmonize at a higher level, although most of us don't realize it's even there beyond random momentary glimpses when we least expect it.

As humans, we are fortunate enough to have the capacity and capability to understand and solve our problems, but we generally fail horribly. As a whole, our very contradictory natures defy simple logic and truth.

We are more than capable of using the tools available to all of us, to teach our children and each other, how to avoid pride, greed, envy, gluttony, wrath, sloth, poverty, war, and chaos, to be able to love and accept each other for the beautifully diverse people we are. But most of us don't see, or don't want to see, that. Whether it's because of socioeconomic reasons, religious dogma, a complete lack of interest, or something somewhere in between, peace and goodwill toward our fellow human is often lacking.

Maybe that's why the remaining one percent eludes us so monumentally; it's probably hiding in plain sight. That vital one percent is the biggest and smallest piece of the puzzle, the key to the universe and everything it contains. But what makes up this one percent? This other level of awareness?

I believe it relates to consciousness and spans the entire timeline of humanity and all the knowledge therein, involving the alpha and omega and everything in between. If not for the one percent, how would any living thing be able to define or determine anything? How would the bees know which flowers to pollinate? What controls the inherent instincts of every living thing? How would we know how to reproduce? How to raise babies? How would animals and birds know how and when to migrate? I believe everything happens for a reason. After all, why would our Higher Power/Source Energy/the Universe make a bunch of random, inconsequential stuff happen? Wouldn't that just be a waste of time, energy, and resources? Yet that is also the 99 percent. A bunch of seemingly random, inconsequential stuff. But it's not random or inconsequential. The one percent is what holds it all together; the common thread.

"Coincidence" is camouflage for the one percent when we don't want to entertain the possibility of things outside of what we can see, hear, and touch. Phenomena like telepathy, premonitions, precognition, ESP, time travel, parallel universes, spiritual awakenings, psychic ability, and so much more are only now starting to be investigated and partially recognized by science.

Although elusive in definition, the one percent clarifies the voice of reason, and even when it is brutal, it is always honest. Much like UFOs—denied for decades, but now the curtain has been pulled back, and we can look if we want to. But that's the thing—only if we want to.

You can lead a horse to water and all that. You could have all sorts of incredible and amazing things happen to you on the regular, but if you cannot find a personal, satisfactory explanation for these events, you are going to deny their existence, closed to the possibility, and probably pick up some bad habits in your attempt to forget them and your feelings about them.

It would further appear that some of us are more in tune with these occurrences, more aware of the elusive nature of consciousness and able to perceive things on that other level.

I think this is inherited, although not every member of my family experiences such events. My own heightened perception seems to have been passed down from my mother, which is known as "second sight," meaning there are two types of sight—our ordinary eyesight (the 99 percent), and then a second type of sight (the one percent) that allows an individual to have prophetic visions and similar other perceptive abilities. It has been proven that if one of your parents has second sight (usually passed down on the mother's side), there is a 50 percent chance you will have it too.

Which leads to the question: Would modern genomic studies confirm these results?[2]

---

2   https://noetic.org/blog/do-psychic-abilities-run-in-families/

An international screening of over 3,000 people was conducted in 2019 by IONS (Institute of Noetic Science[3]), a non-profit research group who use science to explore consciousness. Using tests and interviews, they extracted DNA and sequenced the genes from high-performing psychics and people that did not claim to have psychic abilities.

And they discovered that psychics had one section of their non-coding DNA conserved, also called a "wild-type," which means it was the original DNA and not a mutation or a variant. These were found to be intron DNA (previously considered "junk" DNA and not very important, with all the emphasis being on exon DNA up until that point). It has been discovered that these intron DNA are important because introns control how genes are expressed. This has since opened a new branch of research on DNA and genes and how they affect the individual when it comes to consciousness. By applying scientific methods to the events that make up the one percent and the perception of these things within us, we are starting to better understand our capacities and the role that consciousness plays in the physical world. Which gives some solid validation for the perception of such events. But I think that the one percent is made up of three main components—omniscience, unity consciousness, and love.

There is no escaping the omniscient, all-knowing wisdom that exists in life. Omniscience refers to the quality of having infinite knowledge. It is part of the one percent that connects everyone and everything, long touted to be only a divine or higher power-like ability. I'm not so sure.

---

3 https://noetic.org/about/noetic-sciences/

The very idea raises questions about the nature of knowledge, the limitations of human understanding, and the interconnectedness of it all.

My own experiences, and those I have shared with my daughter, have been quite unnerving at times, but they cannot be denied. Receiving messages that seemingly come from nowhere but are wanting to be understood deep within can be terrifying and confusing. And try as we might, they cannot be ignored.

In religious traditions, the concept of divine omniscience is central to the understanding of a higher power. The idea that a supreme being has perfect and complete knowledge of all things past, present, and future has profound theological implications.

But while human knowledge is limited, the pursuit of wisdom and understanding is a fundamental aspect of our nature. We are driven by a desire to expand the boundaries of knowledge. The idea of omniscience, though apparently unattainable for mortals, serves as a guiding beacon for the relentless pursuit of knowledge.

Which is why I keep trying to see deeper into the one percent, the things that make up the very deepest part of us. And that brings me to unity consciousness, which is a spiritual concept that transcends the boundaries of individualism and shows us the interconnectedness of life. The idea that there is a higher plane of awareness, where everything is intertwined and accessible at the same time, has long been a popular topic of discussion in philosophical circles, even going so far as to delineate into multiple branches of unity consciousness. But the predominant form of unity consciousness and central feature is understood to be as follows:

Unity of consciousness: a group of representations being related to one another so that to be conscious of any of them is to be conscious of all of them and of the group of them as one single group.[4]

It's the events that happen, and the connections we feel, which tap into a deeper knowledge of more significance than the materialistic existence most of us participate in.

A common metaphor of the unity consciousness interconnectedness is the web of existence, wherein each individual, every living being, and all aspects of the universe are interconnected threads of this vast web.

This perspective encourages a broader world view that recognizes the interdependence of all elements of existence. Basically, everything is connected.

Which in its simplest form shows us it all comes back to love. It can be argued that love is the beginning and the end of everything. It is what gives meaning to our most significant thoughts, feelings, and relationships.

Love is the ultimate engagement of unity consciousness. People like Dr. Deepak Chopra have long spoken of the power of infinite love and its effect on every living being.

The central note of love is oneness. Love speaks the language of oneness, and of unity rather than separation. Love can open us to our deep participation in this life of the whole; it can teach us once again how to listen to life, feel life's heartbeat, sense its soul. When you are operating from the level with love in your heart, it keeps you open.

Which in turn exposes us to all those events which seemingly defy logical explanation.

---

4   https://plato.stanford.edu/Archives/sum2005/entries/consciousness-unity/

Once you start looking at it, what you start looking at changes.

I have looked at all of these things from so many angles, and researched and talked to people, and I'm not sure I have even half of the picture. I feel I am getting closer though.

Carolyn, me, and Tim: the think tank.

Me and J. Brannon, the duo known as JohnTe'.

Shirley and Kimberly

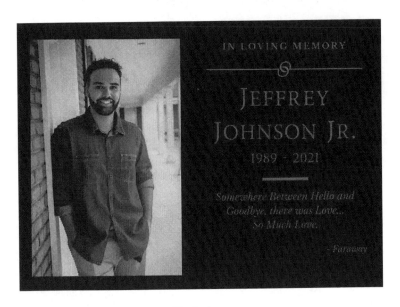

Shirley's son

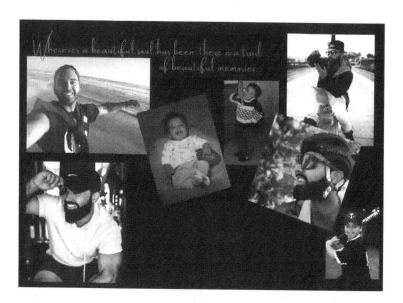

Shirley's son

Tanya, Carolyn, Mom, and Cha

Dante Jr., me, Mom, my wife, and Marquette

Mom's work

Mom's work

Me, Marquette, and the soccer team

Me and Connie; the last time I saw her.

Nikki, Mom, and Tati at Cha's wedding

Eldorado and Habeeba driving school

Diana/Habeeba

Marquette and Dante Jr.

Dantrell. Viva Las Vegas.

Kathy, Mom, and Carolyn in Hawaii

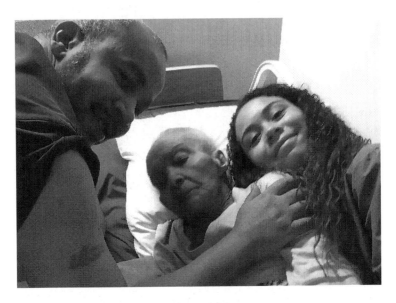

Me, Mom, and Marquette

The twins

Coming Soon

Keen Solomon and the Purple Heart

The future

Made in the USA
Columbia, SC
31 May 2024